Go, Improv

How to improvise your life

Steve Freeto

Dedicated to GoProv Players and Audiences

Published 2020

Cover Design Elijah Durnell
Cover Art Work Benjamin Longcor
Back Cover Photo Mathew Espinosa

D1250412

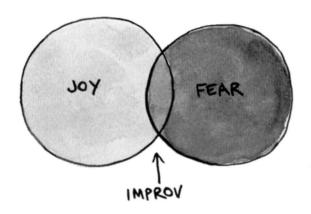

Image credit: Sally Smallwood, People and Chairs Improv

"Life is improv and improv is life. Go, Improv." Steve Freeto, GoProv Founder

"The thing that always fascinated me about improv is that it's basically a happy accident that you think you're initiating." Tina Fey

"Listen, say "yes", live in the moment, make sure you play with people who have your back, make big choices early and often." Amy Poehler

"Smorgity borgity!" Angie Pippenger

"...GoProv is what happens when one man is able to put together an amazing group of improv players" Stephanie Patka Mahoney

"Sorry I didn't make it to your show." Everyone Else

Go, Improv

Chapter 1: Improv is Life (Matt and Tara wedding)

Chapter 2: Guidelines and Fundamentals

Chapter 3: Circle Up

Chapter 4: Aardvark to Zoinks Short Form Games

Chapter 5: Audience Interaction

Chapter 6: Long Form Structure and Medium Form

Chapter 7: Directing

Chapter 8: Performance

Chapter 9: Inclusivity and Diversity

Chapter 10: Do Good Art

Chapter 1

Do you know The Freeto?

As a lifelong fan of pretend, make believe, and play, Steve always loved comedy, laughing, theatre, and performing. Steve attended Second City Chicago for training in improvisation, just long enough to realize that if you want something, you can create it. Seeing a gap in improv comedy in Northern Indiana, Steve founded an improv comedy troupe based in Goshen, Indiana. "Goshen Improv" aka "Improv on the go" became widely known as GoProv.

Steve was the kind of class clown who was also the teacher's pet. Teachers loved Steve. Maybe it was because he didn't have a mom or dad. Maybe Steve was clever, witty, and funny and that's why teachers loved him. Who really knows?

Steve's best friend and biggest GoProv fan tragically died. Life changed after Heidi passed away. Drastic changes... These highlights could be the origin story that no one is asking for at this time.

Ah hell, this isn't an autobiography. Steve loves making people smile. Steve stops talking in 3rd person right about now. I hope you realize that improv is life and life is improv. This book is being shared with lovers of improv, improv performers, improv teams, directors, coaches, and friends of The Freeto. GoProv has had many iterations and various seasons, and show themes:

Survive This (pre-GoProv)

Improv Battle Royale with Cheese

The Big Improvski

Now in Cursive

Brief Questionable Behaviour

Awkward Box Comedy

Fickle Pickle

50 Shades of GoProv

50 Shades Dorkier

Laughing Dead

GayProv

An Improv Spectacular on Ice

Funny Boo Boo

Funny Boo Boo Doublewide

GoProv Saves the Earth

Dazed and Improvised

GhoulProv

August 27, 2016

An improvised wedding toast...ish.

Congrats to Matt and Tara.

As with improv and in marriage there are a few basic rules to follow that will take an ordinary scene/situation to exciting new levels. The first rule of improv is to agree. Matt this is specifically for you. Always agree with Tara, well at least do not deny any request made by Tara. Always say "Yes". Specifically "Yes, Tara." Repeat after me. "Yes, Tara". That is a good start.

The second rule is directly related, so be sure to say "yes, and". Yes, Tara I will take out the trash and I will put a new bag in the can. Not only will Tara be grateful for you taking out the trash, she will also be excited that you know there is more to the job that you will also do. Happy wife. Happy life they say.

One thing that will slow down a scene in improv is asking questions. For marriage, it's simple. Matt do not question Tara. Just follow Tara's lead and agree. Tara knows that her words are a gift and you will be best if you accept the gift and expand and heighten those words.

When on the improv stage and in a marriage you should always make your partner look good...always. Improv is about ensemble. It's about working together to make each other shine. Marriage is great when each person strives to make each other the star. Together your marriage will shine.

Another piece of advice from the world of improv is to stay out of your head. Don't over think and don't get trapped with negative thoughts. Don't let your words outpace your actions and intentions.

Stay positive, stay focused and know that your partner will be there to help you when you flop. Have each other's back, have fun, take care of each other, and attack the stage. Congrats to Matt and Tara.

Ok, now I need a location, a career, an object, or a relationship between two people.
(The audience of wedding guests then yelled out proctologist, dildo, and library-or something like that.)

Chapter 2

Guidelines and Fundamentals

Some of the most common fears that humans have is the fear of public speaking, performing in front of an audience, snakes, and the fear of opening a can of biscuits. These are all valid and reasonable fears. Learning how to improvise will certainly help address all of these fears, especially the biscuit can popping open in your face. Learning the guidelines and fundamentals of performing improv will help reduce those fears. Even after performing in hundreds of improv shows and other performances, I still get that nervous feeling in my gut. It makes me feel alive and excited to get on stage. I hope to always have that nervous excitement to perform. Ideally, any newcomer to improv will have weeks and months of practice and rehearsal before getting on a stage in front of an audience. These guidelines and fundamentals will help create improv performers who have knowledge of the art and the confidence to get out there and make things up.

Improv is a series of scenes or theatre games designed to allow the actor to create and discover characters, settings, situations, and action based on a simple suggestion.

GoProv Common Improv Guidelines

These guidelines have been collected over the years. More like found, borrowed, and stolen from other improvisers through performance, workshops, websites, books, discovery, discussion, and osmosis. These are generally accepted as guidelines followed by all GoProv improvisers.

- To improvise is to expand and heighten the discoveries of the moment.
- Avoid preconceived ideas. Start each improv scene like a blank canvas waiting to be covered with details.
- Always agree; never deny verbal or physical realities.
- Follow the leader, yet lead so that others can follow.
- Move action forward by adding to the last moment, not sideways by trying to wedge your idea into the scene. Explore and heighten.
- Every line should advance the scene forward.
- Don't push a scene. Follow it and add to it.
- You don't have to try to be funny. Laughter will happen.

- Be specific. "Look at this!"-wrong. "Look at this bloated can of biscuits!"-correct.
- Start in the middle.
- Play the opposite.
- Everything is important. Everything matters.
- "Yes, and" is everything.
- "Yes, and" is always better than "No, but" or "No, and" or "Yes, but." Always "yes, and" your partner.
- Be alert. Listen very hard to everything outside of yourself. Listen to the words and actions of the scene.
- Follow your fears; if you are not comfortable with some aspect of your work, try to do it anyway. Your ineptness and courage will be a truer source of entertainment.
- Try not to invent. Try to discover.
- Less is more.
- Show don't tell. Use object work (miming). Trust that the audience will see and they will respect you even more.
- Accept what your partner does or says as a gift, not as a challenge.
- Try not to top somebody until you have equaled them. Share the focus with your scene partner and ensemble.
- Do not ask questions if you can avoid it. Turn the question around and make a statement out of it. Questions put the responsibility on your partner.

- Think on the laughter, talk and move on the silence.
- No scene is ever just about the words that are being spoken.
- To help find an end to the scene, look to the beginning. Come full circle if you can. Circles are everything in improv (spoiler)
- Try to end just before you peak.
- If you are bored, your audience is also bored. This may mean you are not building anything interesting. You can just about do anything to an audience-scare them, disgust them, please them, amuse them-but try to never bore them.

Each one of these guidelines could be a chapter on their own. Really focus on building your improv foundation. You will be a better improviser if you focus on making your scene partner look great and they do the same. Improv is truly about the ensemble and not the individual performer.

New for 2020 (Duh!)
- Don't be an asshole.
- Don't be racist.
- Don't be transphobic.
- Don't be homophobic.
- Don't be ableist.
- Don't be ageist.

- Don't be sexist.
- Don't be a dick.
- Don't make marginalized people the joke.
- Don't touch people without consent.
- Be better or be quiet.
- Do your work to be a better human.
- Do this work outside of the improv space.
- Do address your own "ist" moments and situations.

When you learn these guidelines and rules, know that your scene partner will rely on you to have a basic understanding of how to improvise. Obviously rules are meant to be broken, and it will happen. Never set your partner up to fail. Make each other look good.

Definitions and Terms:

- Accepting - Embracing each offer made by the other players to advance the scene. (Yes, And)
- Advancing - The process of moving a scene forward.
- Endowing - Assigning attributes to another performer's character.
- Focus - The center of attention of the audience. The focus should be in one place at any time.

- Heightening - Adding information, to build upon what was built before and by others, to deepen character and emotion.
- Justifying - Finding a solution for every offer and every element introduced in the scene. The idea is to justify everything.
- Object Work - Miming the objects and props.
- Offer - Any action or dialog that may advance a scene. Offers are supposed to be accepted. A strong offer is an offer that clearly gives a direction into which a scene might evolve.
- Pimp or Pimping – Making an offer or suggestion to another player or the scene that may make the player uncomfortable or in a difficult situation. This is meant in jest and not necessarily a negative. For example endowing a scene mate with character that sings may make the player uncomfortable, especially if that player is not a singer. Used sparingly and usually related to some inside joke or reference.
- Status - A characters sense of self-esteem.

Having an understanding of this information is what will establish a great career in improv. Oh, and good luck having an improv career. Maybe just focus on being passionate and having fun.

You may not want to become an improviser on a stage but you can use some of these exercises, skills, and activities to fulfill your personal and work life. The confidence of knowing that you can make it through any situation by listening, supporting, heightening, and improvising is powerful. Improv can be used day to day in all interactions including the work life or personal life. Job interviews, presentations, and interpersonal connections are so much better with improv. Simply use "yes, and" as a starting point. It's an easy way to collaborate.

Improv is a way to have fun, play pretend, be silly, meet other weirdos, and to learn inter-personal skills. You don't even need a theatre or a stage. You can improvise anywhere. Try it at the grocery store. Use a character to improvise and interact with single serving strangers.

I've met some of my best friends in improv. Sharing smiles and laughs with other humans is wonderful. My circle of friends are either on the stage with me or have been invited to my improv shows. Give away tickets if you can. Fill the audience with people who will laugh at you.

I'm sure you already know this, but you've been improvising your whole life. I'm just offering some structure that helped me.

Go, Improv!

Chapter 3

Circle Up

It's a skill that is learned, practiced and rehearsed.

Everything we do starts with a circle. The strength of a circle and the desire to include everyone in the ensemble is important. Starting in a circle allows each of us to make eye contact and see each other before our backs are up against the wall (quite literally when on stage).

Judy Fabjance, original Gayco ensemble member and my first teacher at Second City broke the ice in her class with this very silly name game. That first moment of my first class helped me realize that letting go and jumping in is vital for improv comedy. (Rest in peace, Judy - f' cancer).

If you have a group of people willing to play improv games, start with these introductions, warm ups, exercises, games, and activities.

Name Game (Get to know each other's name):

Show Us How to Get Down (Ice breaker, Name Game)

Circle up, of course. Everyone share their name (and this would be a good time to also share pronouns). Go around the circle and each person will say someone else's name. "Hey (name) show us how to get down!" That person will say "no way". The entire circle all say "Hey (name) show us how to get down. They will say "ok" and step into the circle, do a little dance and sing "this is how I get down". The entire group will mimic the dance and sing along "D-O-W-N this is how we get down." That person will then challenge someone else in the circle to show how to get down. Just call their name and say "show us how to get down." It's fun! It's silly! It's a great ice breaker. You may remember the dance more than their name.

Group Warm-up (Get everyone ready to play):

Alien Tiger Cow (Focus, Listening)

There are three things that the players can be. The first is an alien. The alien is signified by making antennae with your fingers and leaning into the circle making the noise "zeep zeep zeep". The second thing you can be is a tiger. The tiger is signified by leaning into the circle exposing your ferocious claws and roaring. The last is the cow. The cow's udder is exposed by putting your hand on your stomach and mooing loudly. Someone in the circle quickly counts to three. On three everyone commits to one of the three character types: alien, tiger, or cow. Keep repeating the cycle of 1-2-3 until everyone does the same creature. Generally dissolves into complete chaos before there is any synchronicity.

Bippity Bippity Bop (Focus, Listening)

The person in the center of the circle starts to spin madly. They rapidly count up to ten while spinning around. Once they arrive at the number ten they point to one of the people in the circle. The person pointed at then sticks their arm in front of their face and dangles it like an elephant trunk. The people on either side of the "trunk" must make the ears of the elephant. So the person on the left side uses their left arm to touch their head, and the person on the right uses their right arm to form the right ear. Yes it does look really silly. Meanwhile the dizzy person in the center yells "Bippity Bippity Bop". The elephant must be formed before the center person gets to "Bop". If the elephant does not have ears and a trunk by the time "Bop" is called then someone has to replace the person in the center of the circle. Whichever person is responsible for the part that was not formed by the time "Bop" was yelled has to go into the center. I.e., if the elephant has a trunk and a right ear, but no left ear then the person to the left of the trunk goes into the circle. Ties are decided by someone else from the circle.

Group Exercises (Get everyone involved):

Gibberish Circle (Endowing)

Once in the circle one of the players turns to their left and greets their neighbor in a gibberish tongue. That player responds with a gibberish "hello" that mimics the other player. That player turns around and greets the next in the circle and so on. Once the gibberish greeting has gone around the whole circle the gibberish gets embellished. For instance, all the gibberish could be sad gibberish, or happy gibberish, Italian gibberish, Scottish gibberish, Cantonese gibberish, or computer gibberish. The goal is get people communicating emotions and concepts without depending on words.

Bus Ride (Accepting, Advancing, Character, Endowing, Heightening, Justifying, Status)

Use chairs to build the interior of a bus with rows of 2 and 1 seat at the front for the driver. One player starts driving the bus, and another player becomes a bus rider. The bus rider character has a particular character tick or particular emotion, which the driver takes over. Other riders join in one at a time, each with their own characteristics or emotions, taken over by the driver and the passengers on the bus. Everyone will have the same actions or words.

Group Activities

Advertising Agency (multiple groups) (Character, Advancing, Endowing, Focus, Offer)

Split into small groups. Each group will create a product, define its use and perform a quick commercial for that product. Think infomercials.

Alphabet Circle (2 groups) (Focus, Listening)

Everyone in a circle. One player starts by saying an 'A' to another player. That player throws as fast as possible a 'B' to someone else. And so on. Begin with letters, then words. Split into groups and compete to see who finishes "A" to "Z" first. If not going around the circle, make sure to make eye contact to do a cross circle toss of the letters and words.

Hello (All) (Accepting, Advancing, Endowing, Heightening, Justifying)

All players walk around the room. Greet each other casually. Leader will change greeting styles. "Greet each other as arch enemies", "Greet each other as long lost friends", etc.

Environment Build (Object Work, Heightening, Advancing, Justifying)

This is a silent exercise. An environment is called out at the beginning of the exercise. Each player comes on stage and mimes one object in the environment and leaves the scene. Each following player also adds an object to the environment, but before they do so they must use each mime object previously created within the context of the environment. So the first player has it easy, but the fifth player would have to use all four of the previously mimed objects in the environment before adding theirs. The exercise helps with object work, visual listening, and attention to detail. Commitment is an important component of this exercise because players will often be faced with mime objects that do not make any sense to them at all. It is also informative to have the players tell what each of their objects was once the exercise is over. That way everyone can find out what each player really mimed. Get ready to have a toilet in every scene.

Freeze (Quick thinking, Justification, Accepting)

Two players start a scene. At any given point any player on the back line can yell "freeze" causing the players in the scene to freeze their movement and dialogue. The player who yelled "freeze" will tag out of the scene members taking over the exact position of one of the players; taking the position and starting a new scene and dialogue.

Goalie (Character, Accepting, Justifying)

1 player stand up front. They are the goalie. The other players all think of an opening line and a character. Form a single file line and bombard the goalie with these offers, one at a time. Goalie needs to react right away to an offer, acknowledging the opening and the character,

snap into an opposite character and reply to the opening. Immediately after that the next player comes up with their offer. This exercise is good for teaching players to react to establish a character immediately.

Yes, And (teams of 2) (Accepting, Advancing, Endowing, Focus, Listening, Heightening)

In "Yes, and" the players are constantly saying, "yes, and" after each statement. One player may start off with "Your coat is so lovely." The response of the other player could be, "YES AND I made it for you." The other player responds, "YES AND I have a thousand dollars for it." "YES AND I am going to use that money to make a hundred more coats for you." The players must always have the "yes and" at the beginning of their sentence. This works best if the players truly accept what was said and add onto the suggestion.

Yes Lets (Accepting, Advancing, Endowing, Heightening, Justifying, Object Work)

Someone will loudly suggest an activity for all the group to mime through object work and non-verbal activities. Everyone simultaneously yells "yes lets", and starts to do the activity. Once the activity has been mimed for a while another activity is yelled out and the group responds with "yes lets" and starts the activity. For example, if someone calls out let's all dig holes. The group responds with "yes let's dig holes", and every manner of hole digging mime will begin (complete with sound effects if needed). Then someone will suggest a new activity and the cycle continues.

Zip Zap Zop (Focus, Listening)

The classic theatre and improv warm up game. The phrasing is Zip, Zap, Zop in that order. Pass them one at a time from player to player. One player starts by making eye contact with another player, claps their hands together and slides one hand forward verbally sending the "zip". That person receives it and passes "zap" on to another player. Keep going through the Zip, Zap, Zop. Make eye contact first. Never do this on stage in front of an audience, preshow "green room" warm up is perfect. See the ZoomProv section for a fun variation.

Now that you are all warmed up, get into character and play!

What makes a character?

Realize that you probably aren't as funny as a character you establish in improv. Your character will have a variety of interesting components that will be discovered throughout the scene. Expand and heighten the truth of your character choices.

- Voice: speaking pace, pitch, and accent.

- Attitude: Start with an emotion. Love, Fear, Anger, Sadness, Surprise, Joy (See the Junto Institute Emotion and Feeling Wheel pg 20).
- Physicality/Posture: Capture the energy and the shape.
- Animal: Animal like (base). Be animal like in movement and motivation, not necessarily an animal in character choice.
- Prop: Symbol or object of who/how we feel.
- Obsession/knowledge: what we know.
  - Do what you know and know what you do.
    - Bring in your knowledge and references.
    - Make it up. You are right, regardless of how wrong you are. Believe in your delivery.
- Conflict doesn't always have to be an argument between two or more.
  - Human vs Human (argument or fight)
  - Human vs world (tackle big issues)
  - Human vs society (outer thoughts)
  - Human vs themselves (inner thoughts)
  - Human vs nature (ahh, bear attack)
  - Human vs technology (these dump phones)
  - Human vs supernatural (ghosts?)
- There is no punishment for failure. Know you are right. Know you are good. We all support each other.

- Listening is more than ears. Watching, perceiving, reacting, and sensing with your whole being by completely taking in your scene partners and the space around you.
- You are always in the scene. Even when not on the stage.

So many emotions...spin the wheel explore that emotion. Be more than happy/horny/angry. Get in touch with those feelings!

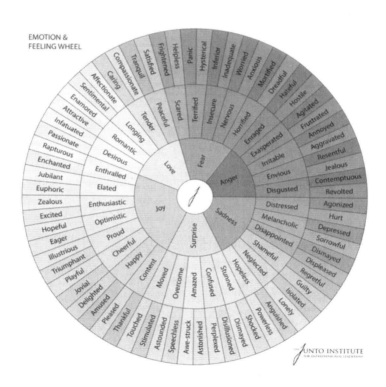

EMOTION & FEELING WHEEL

Chapter 4

185 Aardvarks to Zoinks

(A collection of short form improv games)

Short form improv is a style of performance using theatre games and short scenes. These are usually a couple minutes long. Pick some games and put together your very own improv show.

185

The audience provides random nouns to be included in a ridiculous statement made by the players. It's an assumption that a group of 185 somethings can enter the world's most exclusive bar. One player uses that noun in a very specific structure: 185 _____'s walk into a bar, the bartender says "I'm sorry, but we don't serve _____'s here". Player supplies the pun or punchline retort to the bartender. An example: 185 Aardvarks walk into a bar. Bartender says "We don't serve aardvarks here" and the 185 aardvarks say "Just looking for our aunts."

Puns are horribly hilarious and a sign of intelligence. Moans and groans are good for an improv show! Put this at the top of the show and "get the puns out of the way". Follow the format and structure of the set up to allow yourself time to think of a terrible...well a good pun.

3 Headed Broadway Star

Three players will sing a song from a fake Broadway show. Seek an audience suggestion of a yet to be produced Broadway musical. Each "head" will sing one sentence at a time. The group will create the chorus.

Shoulder to shoulder creating one "monster" with 3 heads is always funny, looking.

90 Second Alphabet

Head to head battle between two teams of two to see who can complete A to Z the fastest (or less than 90 seconds). Get a scene suggestion and a random letter from the audience. Start the scene with each consecutive sentence starting with the next letter of the alphabet. Finish at the starting letter.

The pressure of being quick and quick witted often leads to a new version of the alphabet, embrace it. Laugh at the fact that most of us aren't as smart as we think.

A1 Freeze Tag/Blind Freeze

Two players start. One player asks the audience for a letter of the alphabet and the other player asks for a number between 1 and 9. The players move their bodies into the shape of the letter or number that was provided. Begin a scene from those postures and poses. Other players will yell "freeze", tapping out a player, assuming their position, and starting an unrelated scene. Variation: Blind Freeze where players will face the back wall and yell freeze without seeing what is happening.

Use it at the end of the show, include an audience member. Just be sure to freeze the audience member before they ruin the night.

Actors Nightmare
Using a variety of scripts from a play, movie, tv show, or any printed documents will work. One player (or sometimes both) must only use dialogue from the source material. Flip through quickly to find relevant, related, funny, or connected lines of dialogue. The other players must justify what is being stated.

This is more difficult than it seems, add a third unscripted player to fill in the space while the person on the script finds the right words.

Adjective Scene/Emotions
Start a scene with any audience suggestion of either a location or a relationship. The host will pause the scene. At that point, the host will ask for an emotion or an adjective to offer for the players to change the scene based on that suggestion.

This is good to increase the interaction with the audience. Get them involved. Audiences love to take credit for the laughs. Asking for suggestions helps solidify the idea that it's all made up.

Arms Expert
2 players play a scene while 2 other players supply the "arms" of the players. The players hide behind other players while providing arms of those players.

Angels/Devils

2 players tell a story, taking turns. One storyteller, playing (The Angel) starts with some good, positive things like, "Once upon a time Mary had a beautiful little lamb." Then the other storyteller (The Devil) tells the next part of the story, but it is all negative (acceptance is still vital), so, "Unfortunately, the lamb had a peg leg." The Angel storyteller, "Fortunately, Mary opened the leg and the lamb was filled with chocolate." Other player: "Sadly, lamb chocolate was illegal in Greece, where they lived, and Mary and the lamb were sent to farmer's prison." As a variation, two other players could mime out the story as it happens. Do not deny your partner, just be the "Debbie Downer".

Always try to expand and heighten this one. It gets weird.

Audience Text

Borrow a phone from a willing audience member. One player can only speak using texts from the audience phone. Other player must justify what is said. Variation of Actors Nightmare.

"B" Movie

Get 1 noun from the audience. Players tell about a "B" movie about (noun) that was so bad...Audience responds with "How bad was it?" The player answers with a pun or punchline related to the noun. I saw a B movie about Chickens that was so bad. How bad was it? It was so bad, I wanted to cross the road.

Puns for the win! Get the audience involved in shouting the "how bad was it?"

Ballad of an Audience Member

Two contestants sing a ballad about an audience member.

This works best with guitar or keys or someone with enough talent to sing.

Battle Scene

One team leaves the stage area while the other team performs a scene. That team does not watch or listen to the 2-3 minute scene. After the scene ends the other team gets the opportunity to perform a scene using the same audience suggestion.

If you and your team can go first, it will be more difficult for the other team, especially if the audience is laughing. Just make the audience howl with laughter.

Beastie Rap

There is this guy, his name is Steve. When it's time to play this he would leave. He has no rhythm and no rhyme. He messes up every occasion.

Best Actor

Each player is a nominee for the Best Actor Award to some made up awards show. The audience provides the title of the movie and each actor must perform a scene from that movie. The audience votes on best actor (applause). The actor will give their award speech.

This is a fun way to get the group working together and give a monologue opportunity for one of the players.

Blues Jam

Sing a blues song based on audience suggestion

Get a musician...start singing "Woke up this morning..."

Bucket/Slips of Paper

Audience provides sentences pre-show and those sentences are used in the scene. Players will stuff their pockets with the papers and will pull them out during a scene to use as the next line of dialogue.

Your preshow interaction with the audience will help get the audience invested. Either have someone elicit the suggestions or have a really clever sign for the

> *audience to write stuff. Be careful, it will turn dirty thanks to anonymity.*

Bucket of Water

One player will submerge their head under water in bucket while other players do a scene. When the player can't handle being under water any further, they tap the floor until one player justifies leaving a scene and tap out the bucket head who enters the scene (wet).

> *On second thought this is kinda gross. I can't believe GoProv has done this multiple times.*

Chair

2 players/1 chair. One player has to remain seated and the other has to justify a reason for that player to get up. When the seated player stands, the other player takes the seat. Similar to sit/stand/kneel but with 2 players.

> *A boring audience will give principal and student relationship if you let them. Get creative.*

Close Up/Long Shot

Random scene is played as "close up" using whole body and when the host calls out "long shot" the scene is played with fingers (hands) as the miniature characters in the scene. Think of this like a camera on a film set. Shooting close up or from far away.

> *Long shots are the perfect time to jump in the air and do flips to prompt the host to switch to close up.*

Coffee House

Players are given an object, and must perform a short poem, monologue, or "skat" about said object. Each player can perform alone, or the other players can assist by giving some background "music".

Offer finger snaps like a beatnik in a coffee house from the 50's.

Couples

Two contestants improvise a scene changing into various famous couples as suggested by the audience.

Don't worry about gender roles. Just play. Get iconic characters and couples.

Cutting Room Floor

2 Players are actors and 1 is a director. Play the scene and follow the suggestions of the director. Yell "cut" and change the scene. New genre, switch roles, add action, and make it better!

This is one of the chances to stop the scene and figure out a way to make it better. Get the audience involved.

Day in the life

An audience member shares an embarrassing day in their life. Thank the audience member and replay that scene.

Make the audience member look awesome. Do not make them the joke or mock them. Reward them for volunteering by improving their past life. An audience on your side will come back to your shows.

Die

All players form a line facing the audience. The audience suggests a general product category (candy bars, cars). No doubles are allowed, neither are existing brand names. A player that makes a mistake "dies". Play until only one player is left standing.

Make it rapid fire and force the players to commit to something. Last one standing wins.

Ding (New Choice, Say it again, say what)

The scene is played and the previous line is stated in a different way with each ding of the bell. Continue the scene with the replacement words or actions.

Use a bell to ding or you can also verbally call out one of the variations if you do not have a bell. Ding dialogue, action, or content of the scene. Rapid fire dings are always funny to the audience.

Do Run Run

Single syllable name from the audience. Sing/rap a rhyme to that name. Example: Player 1: I once met a man named Joe. All: A do run run a do run run. Player 2: He was always on the go. All: A do run run a do run run. Player 3: Hey, I met him at the show. Player 4: Hey, we went to and fro. Player 5: Hey, he was friends with Sheryl Crow. All: A do run run a do run run. Continue in rhyming pattern.

Practice this over and over. Actually it does get a little boring to do on stage too much.

Duet

2 Players sing a song about an audience member.

> Would be great with a musician to provide a beat. Interview the audience member and make them the focus of the song. Always make the audience member feel safe and the hero of the scene.

Edit

The Scene is edited by the host. Jump in time, add characters, any edit is possible.

> This is a good chance to read the audience, pause the scene and make a change. Switch performers, add action, add emotion, change genre, or whatever you think.

Emotions

Play a scene and freeze to add an audience provided emotion, continue the scene.

> Similar to edit and directors cut but focus on emotions to pause the scene and get creative. Use the Juntos chart to stop randomly or have the audience suggest something. The audience will probably suggest amorous or horny.

Evil Twin

4 players. 2 will play a scene. The other players are the other's evil twins. At any point, the twins can shout "Evil Twin" after which they tag out their twin and continue the scene and do something evil. After that, they move out again and the original twin needs to

justify the evil, correct or repair the damage done and continue the scene.

> *This is really fun especially with an escalation of "evil". The opposite of this would be "Stunt Double" where the original performers get the scene to the point where they call for their stunt double to take over.*

Excuses

One player leaves the room. The host gets a series of suggestions that all add up to the excuse the vacant player is going to give to their boss to explain why they were late to work. 1. Where they were? 2. What problem did they encounter? 3. How they solved it? 4. What mode of transportation did they use to get to work? The boss will ask leading questions to get the correct answers and any remaining players can act out the suggestions behind the back of the boss to provide clues.

> *Having the audience in on a series of secrets makes it fun to see a player squirm under pressure. This is not a gibberish scene.*

Film, TV, Book Styles

The audience provides styles of movie, tv, or book. The scene begins normal and is changed to match the stated movie, tv, theater style as determined by the host.

> *Also known as "genres". Change it up and get the audience involved to create.*

First Date Gibberish

As the title indicates, this is a half gibberish game. Audience provides: 1. Nonphysical attribute or reason to find someone attractive. 2. Location to go on a date. 3. Reason to break up with someone. Each of the 3 items are conveyed from one player to another using gibberish. Send one player out the room who will enter the scene to console their friend who was just dumped. They are wailing and crying in gibberish. The other player does not speak in gibberish.

Gibberish games require a lot of object work, big physical expressions and patience.

First Line/Last Line

Two teams of two play two separate scenes. Get an opening line of dialogue from the audience to start one of the scenes. The second team will clap in or ring a bell to start a new unrelated scene. The second scene will start by using the last line of dialogue from scene 1. The players from the first scene will clap in or ring a bell to reconvene their scene by using the last line of dialogue used by the second scene. Each scene will continue back and forth. Each team should offer lines of dialogue that are relevant to both scenes, allowing each team the opportunity to restart their scene. Keep the scenes unrelated and distinct, but find ways to get in and get out of the scene.

This is a GoProv favorite. Can even be done with more than 4 players. It's a great way to practice those listening skills.

Five Things

One player leaves the stage while the host asks for an everyday activity. Then, the audience and host will change 5 things about that activity. Example: suggestion is feeding the cat. Change the following: the cat into a tiger, the verb into another verb like "deep frying", change or add the location, change the character to random profession and add interaction with a famous person. Bring back the first person and play the scene in Gibberish. The other players have 5 minutes to make the first person guess each of the 5 things.

> This is another game that the audience is in on the secret answers. Watching the players try to figure out what is going on is always hilarious for the audience. The show is truly about the audience. Get them involved often. Also, don't deep fry a tiger.

Foreign Film

2 players play a story in Gibberish while 2 others translate. The idea is to build the story together. The "actors" give elements to the translators, and the translators can help control the action for the "actors".

> Be careful with stereotypes and accents regarding "foreign". See Xenophobia.

Four Corners

Players form a square (2 upstage and 2 downstage forming a square shape from an overhead view) each pair of players have specific scenes and characters to portray. The host will rotate the players clockwise; changing the scenes to match the other pair. When a scene is rotated, it is paused until back on that scene again. Rotate forward and reverse.

> *Get very distinct character/scene suggestions. Move forward and reverse often to find the funny or interesting moments.*
> *Top view*
> *A   B*
> *C   D*
> *A&B, C&A, D&C, D&B, back to A&B*

Free Association/Reincorporation
Players free associate images related to an audience single word suggestion for 30 seconds providing disconnected phrases and images. Opposing team plays a scene or tells a story based on the free association using as many images as possible. The challenge is to wrap the images into a story and not just say the phrases. Be inspired by the suggestions.

> *Get a chalk board, dry erase, paper or something big enough for the audience to see. The Goshen Art House stage has a back wall that is a great chalk board like surface. Get your own Art House.*

Freeze-I Can Do Better
Start a scene and any player can freeze the scene and say "I can do better"...while describing what you can do

better at while maintaining the scene. It's freeze just with a continuing scene instead of new scenes.

> *"Freeze. I can do better at writing a book about improv..."*

Fusillade

All players line up in 2 lines facing each other. Host yells a word/title and the next player in line gets up to 15 seconds to do something based on the suggestion. Can be pairs or solo performances.

> *A rapid fire friendly competition.*

Genres

The audience provides a variety of genres of movies, tv, theater and with each ding of the bell the host will change the genre.

> *Audiences love Bromance and Porn...but who doesn't?*

Gibberish Expert

One player is giving a lecture on a subject provided by the audience. The expert is from a made up country and needs a translator for the lecture.

> *There's a fun little pimp of saying one word in gibberish and translating into a paragraph or vice versa. Also, Xenophobia is not tolerated. There are many X words, this just happens to be one of the important ones. You will learn how in future chapters.*

Good Bad Ugly

3 Players form a line. The audience provides questions or problems for which they need advice. The players provide good, bad, and ugly (really bad) advice. Players provide characters that stay with the good, the bad, and the ugly position. After each round of answers, the players will rotate through those positions moving to the next position for the second and third question.

> *It works best when "good" is indeed good and "ugly" is so terrible and cringey. When rotating between positions, keep the character where it originated and try to mimic that character already established.*

Good Cop/Bad Cop

Get a common household item that is in need of repair. Player one calls for repair. Repair people show up and use all of the troupes of good cop/bad cop to find the problem and solution.

> *All cops are bastards...don't play this anymore.*

Half Life (60,30,15...)

Two players play a 60 second scene. After 60 seconds, replay the entire scene in half the time. Repeat as much as possible, making sure all highlights of the scene are included in each replay of the scene.

> *The most memorable version of this was at the Sauk Theatre in Jonesville, Michigan (remember it's Improv on the Go). Kilmer and I ended each half life scene with the phrase "I love being married to you, man!"*

Hall of Justice

Get 4 suggestions/nouns from the audience. Examples: hammer, coffee, thong and briefcase. This will give 2 superheroes: Hammergirl and sidekick Coffeewoman. We will also have 2 villains: Thongman and partner BriefcaseWoman. The other players play the victims or bystanders. Villains and heroes should try to use as many attributes of their suggestion as they justifiably can.

If the audience doesn't seem responsive, the first player in can endow the next player with the superhero name.

He Said/She Said (or any pronouns)

Each player will state the action the other player must perform, followed by their own line.

Player 1: "I want a divorce"

Player 2: "She said, while grabbing a knife." At this point, player 1 needs to have a knife. 2 responds to the first line "I will not divorce you, it's against my beliefs".

Player 1: "He said while dropping to his knees to beg"

Player 2 will drop to their knees...Rotate back and forth.

Try to outdo each other with the actions. Expanding and heightening.

Hesitation

It's like Mad Libs but with an audience. Hesitate mid-sentence and have the audience provide next word.

Teach the audience early to use their intelligence and accept words that help establish the scene.

Hidden Word Environment

Two members of a team leave the stage area. The audience provides an environment and three words which might be used in that place. When the team re-enters, they are only given the environment and they begin a scene while trying to discover the three words.

This is one of those "medium form" scenes. Suggestions depend on the audience and their suggestions. Play the scene out and see what develops. It's a good break from short form games. Mix up your set list.

Highlander

Based on the 1986 movie of the same name and the iconic quote "there can be only one". Play a scene with 4 performers. Use any suggestion for something with lots of action and movement for everyone. A scene with 4 talking heads is boring and even more so with 3 talking heads or 2 talking heads. Find the action and make it big. Let the scene develop for a minute or so and then eliminate one of the players. The 3 remaining players will have to replay the entire scene accounting for the words and actions of the missing player. Eliminate and repeat until there is indeed only one. Replay the solo scene with the remaining player accounting for all of the dialogue and action.

This is so much fun to do! Play some Queen music if you can and make sure the scene is full of action. Also, watch the movie if you do not understand the Queen reference. It's great if there is a "cliff hanger" at the end of the first scene that somehow gets resolved in the final scene.

Horoscope
A scene is played based on the horoscope of an audience member. Each player gets a horoscope and uses that for their motivation. Ask an audience member for their birthdate. Read their horoscope and play a scene based on that horoscope.

Find an app or the newspaper or a source that provides interesting and colorful messages. This can also work with tarot cards. Once again, if you find an audience member willing to share and participate, it will be fun.

Inner Dialogue
Play a scene and offstage voices create the inner dialogue for each player. The inner voice will inspire and motivate the players to have the gift of knowledge and insight.

Best if you have a mic. Be sure to play slow to allow time for those thoughts to be spoken by the offstage voices and processed by the onstage players.

I Object
Start a monologue. One player will state "I object" to a specific portion of the monologue and will have to convince the mediator/arbiter/judge why they object. Mediator will either sustain or overrule the objection. Continue the scene. Audience suggestion: dinner time. Player 1 monologue: "Ah yes, dinner time. Let's talk

about side dishes first. "Peas are the best side dish" Player 2: "I object, your honor. We all know that peas have been rated by Side Dish Weekly as the second favorite side dish to tator tots". Judge "Sustained". Player 2 then takes over the scene: "Tator tots are the best side dish..." If overruled by the mediator/arbiter/judge player 1 will continue.

> *Say "I object" to the most unusual parts of the monologue and justify why you are objecting. Treat the scene like a courtroom setting in all of the familiar ways.*

Keyser Soze (Usual Suspects reference)

One group of performers improvise a 60 second scene that is actually the dramatic end of complete 3 minute scene. Think of it as a short 3 act play with a beginning, middle, and an end. The second group will perform Act 1 and Act 2 to justify what happened in the already established Act 3. The second group will then also recreate Act 3. Each act is one minute long. This should be an epic short film.

> *This is a GoProv created game but only played only once or twice. Try it out, master it. Make magic. Tweet at me if you figure this out and do it well @thefreeto*
>
> *Also, we know the actor who played this character is cancelled.*

LCD

Three players. One is on stage and 2 others are sent off stage. The audience provides three unrelated suggestions: a location, an occupation and an object (of death). The second player enters and a scene is played in gibberish. Player one needs to communicate the three words to player 2. When the player understands or guesses the location, they indicate by clapping hands and spinning around (or whatever is decided by your group to communicate). Keeping guessing until the career and object is guessed. Player 2 will then "kill" player 1 with the object. Repeat with player 2 conveying the L, C, D to player 3. After player 3 guesses and kills player 2, reveal the Location, the Career, and the (object) of Death. LCD.

It can be hilarious if done well. When the audience is in on the fun, they enjoy it more. As a player, listen to the audience, especially if it is going too long. If you have no clue what is being done/said, just move on unless the audience is rolling with laughter. This is a GoProv favorite, for both players and audiences. Our dear friend Pipp first used the iconic "Smorgity Borrigty" in this game. This is a GoProv pop culture reference. This will be on the quiz.

Lounge Singer

Seek an audience suggestion for a location and a random profession. A lounge singer will sing a song using those suggestions.

Find a way to include the audience. Get someone on the stage to find their occupation, etc. Sing!

Marriage Counsel
One player, the therapist is sent out of the room while the host gets 2 relationship problems from the audience. Two other players play a couple with these problems. The players need to get the therapist to figure out what the relationship problems are for each person.

Guessing games are always fun, especially when including the audience. Have the audience make some groan or noise when the player is close to guessing the issue. Try to manage the audience suggestions...they will probably mention mostly sex stuff. Mostly Sex Stuff is the name of the book you actually want me to write.

Marshmallow Mania
Players have a bag/bowl of marshmallows and perform a scene. Anytime a player gets a laugh from the audience that player must put a marshmallow in his/her mouth and continue the scene.

Chubby bunny if you went to camp. Don't forget a trash can if you are one who spits. You can always get an audience member involved in this too.

Medley from a Musical
Unlikely name of a musical and song titles. Perform a medley from that musical.

Singing scenes can be fantastic, or the opposite of fantastic. Sing loud and proud.

Modern Fairytale

Get a movie genre from the audience and a favorite fairy tale. Re-tell that story using the provided genre.

Die Hard is already a Christmas movie, but a Lifetime Movie Channel version of Die Hard would be epic. Little Red Riding Hood the stoner movie was hilarious for our audience once.

Movie Review

Ask the audience for a fictional movie title. 2 players will be the reviewers and 2 players will re-enact the scenes discussed.

Siskel & Ebert is a dated reference. Look it up on YouTube. Welcome back. Do that, but funny.

Moving Bodies

Speaking players in the scene cannot move their own bodies - other players are movers who move them around. Works best if the body movers are audience volunteers.

Maybe a touching game is not a good idea any more.

No P

Players play a scene but they cannot use the letter "P" in an part of a word (or any other letter as suggested). They can change the sound or change the word, but the letter cannot be spoken. When a player uses a "P", the audience yells "die" and the player is replaced by another one. The scene continues, and the new player needs to take over the character of the player they replace.

> *Or any other consonant you choose. Let the audience get involved.*

Party Quirks

One Player plays a character that is having a party. Send them away while you ask for quirks for the remaining players (guests). Each guest will knock on the door to enter the party. The game is over when all of the quirks have been guessed by the host. When a quirk is guessed, that guest can take a seat and hang out at the party.

> *Classic short form game. Let the party host spend some time setting up the party. Putting out the snacks, the White Claw and giving the gift of what kind of party will give fodder for the incoming folks. Nothing like a "I have an STI and I have to tell all of my ex-lovers party". Sounds gross but the audience loves gross stuff.*

Picture Slideshow

Each team will have to tell a story using a "slide show". Players freeze into various positions while the presenter justifies each "slide" to tell a story. The slides are established behind the presenter and they will turn around to see what is on display in the slide.

> *Go on vacation or share pics from your imaginary camera just make it creative and interesting. The presenter can mess with the players especially when they are frozen in uncomfortable positions. Hand*

stands held a long long time is a fun way to get cheap laughs.

Pillar

Put one member of the audience on the stage (the pillar). A two person scene is played, but each player can at any point stop mid-sentence and ask the pillar to provide the next word. This is similar to Hesitation but the audience member is on the stage.

Teach the audience member to listen and not try to be funny. They just need to say a word to fill in the blank. Some audience members think it's to swear. GoProv often writes a small list of word not to say.

Pimp Freeze

Freeze tag but the person yelling "freeze" is the pimp that sends someone else into the scene. The player going in will choose who to tag out.

Or any variation of freeze is fun to play. Freeze is a good game to include audience members and any special guests in the crowd. Play at the end of the show. It's a great closer filled with energy.

Press Conference

One player leaves the room while the audience provides the name of a famous or historical person. The absent player will give a press conference, but does not know who they are when they start the press conference. The other players are journalists, whose questions should provide indication as to who is having the meeting.

> Guessing games help the audience participate without having the audience on the stage. Celebrities doing unique things is typical. Have the audience cheer or jeer when the player is getting hot or cold in the guessing.

Puns (Sex w/us, 185, B Movie, Hey Morty, I call my sweetie)

The basic premise is to turn nouns into a punchline: Example: toothbrush-sex with us is like a toothbrush, its better if you use your mouth...185 toothbrushes walk into a bar and the bartender says, we don't serve toothbrushes here and the toothbrushes say "we just wanted a checkup, guess we will come back in 6 months", I saw a B movie about toothbrushes that was so bad (the audience says "how bad was it?") it was rated G for gingivitis., Hey Morty did you hear the one about the toothbrush? It was bristling!

> Yay! Puns are the best.

PSA

Two or more players begin a scene that is meant to look like a public service announcement or an after school special. They try their best to make it not funny. If anyone in the audience laughs, the person that caused the laugh is replaced by someone else.

> A very special episode of improv...an overly dramatic presentation of a silly public service announcement.

Questions Only

Any sentence used by the players must be a question. Any player who does not use a sentence as a question must be replaced by another player on the team. The new player is to take over the character of the player replaced and pick up where the player left off.

> *Aren't questions bad for scene work? Why do people use questions instead of statements? Why does this work so well? Why do audiences like it when a player screws up? Who really is The Freeto?*

Radio Call In

There are two principle players; a host of a radio talk show, and a special guest. Typically, the special guest is the author of a best-selling book, the title of which is suggested by the audience. The remaining players are "callers" that will call into the show to ask the author questions (perhaps about the book, perhaps not). Between callers, the host will also interview the author.

> *A classic. Let an audience member ask questions too.*

Radio Station

Each player will ask the audience for a topic to sing about and a "genre" of music for each "station". House lights will dim and the host will shine a large spot light or flashlight at each player to change the station. Player will sing about the topic in the style. Example: Q1: What is your favorite back to school item? Answer: Pencil. Q2: What music do you hear when your alarm goes off in the morning? Answer: Blues. Player then announces their channel. "I will be singing the blues about pencils". Each station is established and ready for the host to change from station to station.

> *Know the comfort level and singing ability of each player. Help set them up to look good. Singing scenes can really suck unless you let the talent shine where it is brightest. Don't forget to support your local NPR station.*

Rhymes

Scene played in verses. Player 1 offers a line that player 2 must rhyme to complete a couplet. Player 2 offers another line that player 1 must rhyme. Must build a story and pass back and forth. If a player hesitates or forgets to rhyme, another player jumps in. Players die and cannot come back in. The game is over with the last team standing, or it can be played without being a team competition.

> *It's not meant to be a poem just rhymes. Tell a story using rhyming and couplets.*

Short Cuts

This is a free form scene full of "long form edits". A scene will begin and any other edits can be made. You can tap out, time hop, change location, add elements, or just wipe the scene completely. Just play with it to adjust the scene as needed. Let the audience make some decisions.

> *Have the host pause the scene, make the edits, and change things up. Give the audience what they didn't know they really wanted.*

Shut up Donnie

Send away players, the host gets a scene suggestion and 5 related words to that suggestions. Players return and are given the scene suggestion. When one of the hidden words is stated the audience yells "Shut up Donnie". Continue playing until all 5 words are stated. Set a time limit just in case the audience is obtuse.

> *GoProv did this during The Big Improvski era. Try it, adjust as needed, change the name. Do whatever you wish. If the audience can handle it, call it Shut the fuck up Donnie. See the Big Lebowski movie if haven't.*

Sing It (That sounds like a musical/song)

Do a normal scene. At any time the host can tell the players to stop and "Sing It" and the last line of dialogue begins a song.

> *Play to the talents of the group, or make them uncomfortable. Works best with a musician accompanying the players. Singing games are listed throughout this book. When Aaron, Alex, Adam, Geoff, Hannah, and Emily were doing GoProv shows, they would make singing scenes look so easy.*

Sit/Stand/Kneel Xtreme

Get whacked in the head if more than one person is sitting, standing or kneeling at the same time as another player.

> *The classic Sit/Stand/Kneel is made extreme by adding some pool noodles to the effort. The players must maintain one of the three positions at all times or face the pain of a foam smack to the head. Find a willing audience member or two to do the whacking.*

Slow Genius

Three players are seated on stage and are asked "imponderable" questions. They answer together, trying to all say the same thing at the same time.

> *This is the way to lead so others can follow and follow so others can lead. It's not easy and not always funny.*

Soap Opera Extreme

The players give a bell to an audience member. Every time the audience member rings the bell one of the characters will kiss or slap someone.

> *Alright, this is a terrible idea. Don't give that much control to the audience and don't play a scene where there is kissing. Consent is the most important aspect of any scene with physical contact.*

Space Jump

This game will consist of a series of different scenes; 5 scenes works really well. The first scene will have one player, the next will have two players, and so on. At some point in the one player scene someone will yell freeze, and the next person will jump in, justify the position, and start a new scene. This will continue until all five players are in the scene. At that point the players will leave in the reverse order that they came in. As the players leave, the audience will see all the previous scenes taking place as if time had passed, and justifying their new physical positions. This is just a simple game of freeze. The twist to this version is that you must justify the positions of several other people when you start your scene. When the scene includes all five players, the fifth player must find some reason to exit the scene, preferably within the context of the scene. Then the fourth scene spontaneously starts, and the fourth player finds a reason to leave, and the third scene starts and so on.

This is a GoProv favorite. Make sure the scenes are unrelated and definitely make sure the last player in remembers to find a reason to leave the scene. We've had players forget to leave. It's embarrassing for them.

Spelling Bee

Each player is given a made up word by the audience. The player must spell this word and give its definition. The judge can decide who spells correctly.

It's Putnam County Spelling Bee, the improv version.

Starting with the letter

Each player gets a letter of the alphabet and can only use that letter to start each sentence of their scene. A variation would be to start the next sentence with the last letter of the last word of the prior sentence.

> *Big tip...learn "X" words.*

Story Die

Players form a line on the stage. A title for a story and a story genre is obtained from the audience. The host starts the game by pointing to a player, who needs to start telling the story. At any point in time, the host can switch to another player, who needs to continue the story flawlessly or die. The host is the conductor of the story, pointing and directing.

> *Have the audience yell "die" when someone stammers, slowly transitions, or messes up the flow.*

Survival of the funniest

Audience members share a NERF-style toy gun and shoots at a player who is being boring. If hit that player leaves the scene. The funniest will survive the scene.

> *Ok, this was only done once but it was damn fun. Dance, monkey, dance. Try it!*

Superhero

The audience gives a bizarre name for a super hero. That super hero is then on watch in the hall of justice. Another player walks on stage and the first player names them. They interact and more players come on, each being named in turn by the player who came on before them. The Superheroes can work together to solve a problem.

> *Bizarre, obtuse, unusual, and weird superhero names are expected. Identify a problem in the world, and solve it. It's literally that easy to solve all of the world's problems through improv.*

Superhero Eulogy
Give the eulogy of the dead superhero. Provided by sidekick, friends, nemesis.

> *Follow up the Hall of Justice scene with this. Death can be hilarious.*

Sounds like a musical
Players will perform a scene and will burst into song as prompted by the bell or the host declaring "hey that sounds like a musical".

> *The most classic improv music game. Hey, that sounds like a musical.*

Top Ten List
Audience provides a topic for a top ten list either pre-show or during the scene (i.e. Top Ten Ways to Eat a Pie or Top Ten Least Popular grooming items). Players step out and say the current number, and give the number whatever thing on the list.

> *A rapid fire line game good for the stage or for rehearsal. Keep Letterman's legacy alive. Remember to start at 10 and end with a drumroll before #1.*

Translator
Gibberish translation.

> *Translate gibberish. Use a press conference format or a regular scene. Once again, don't be Xenophobic.*

Tweet Speak

Get a twitter name (public account) or a popular twitter celebrity from the audience. One player must only read tweets and the other player must justify. Twitter rants could be good for a full scene.

> *Kinda like "Actors Nightmare" or this can also be done like "lines from a bucket" using tweets for random dialogue.*

Waiter

Prepare by getting audience members to write nouns (including specific places, people, etc.) on slips of paper. One player sits at a table with a soup bowl full of the slips of paper. The other players line up as waiters. The "customer" pulls a slip of paper out of the bowl and says "Waiter, I've got a (noun) in my soup." Someone steps out of the line and utters a witty one-liner response. Repeat until out of paper or booed off stage.

> *Puns! Get suggestions from the audience before the show. Be careful if you allow the audience to write anonymous words, you'll just end up with the dirtiest suggestions. Take it or leave it.*

Weird Newscasters

A news anchor has a co-anchor, sports/finance reporter and weather/traffic reporter with strange quirks. This is not a quirk guessing scene.

Don't do too many party quirks, weird newscasters or other quirk game scenes in one show. These are all similar. Make sure your audience doesn't give ableist quirks. Teach them that Tourette's is not a joke.

World's Worst

The troupe will stand on the back line awaiting suggestions from the audience. When the host gets various suggestions for jobs, careers, etc., one performer at a time will step forward and share the world's worst version of that suggestion.

Line game that goes back to the origin of improv...world's worst bus driver or teacher will be suggested.

You, Idiot

Combination of "props" and "world's worst". All players line up, first player grabs a random prop and describes an unlikely use for it. The next player takes it from the other player and says "you idiot, that's not a...it's a..." Continue through all players

Line games help get all the players involved. Find some props around your space, you idiot.

Zones

Split the stage into quadrants. Each zone has one distinct characteristic that has to be embodied when the characters are in that zone.

> *Make the zones distinct. Physical action, emotion, or a specific character trait.*

Go, Improv!

Improv belongs to all of us. Use these as your own. We borrowed many of these and changed the "rules" to fit our troupe. Do what you will to have fun! Pay it forward. Share this book.

All of these scenes and games can be modified as needed to accommodate your group. As you can tell by some of the descriptions, find a way to get your audience involved in the show. A short form improv comedy show can be highly entertaining if the audience provides enough energy for the players to be excited and everyone is involved in the performance. The host of the show can really set the tone and help both the audience and the performers have a fantastic time. Improv is an interactive art form. Practice, rehearse, play, and share improv.

What happens when a pandemic forces the entire world to shut down? No theatres, no schools, no large gatherings, and no improv...Improv may not be a priority in those situations, however remember "Improv is life and life is improv" Get some wifi, get a web based app and zoom a zoom zoom and boom boom...there you go. It's a good distraction from the pandemic, but really health and safety is more important than improv.

ZOOMPROV

An online Web/Video/Zoom improv session to work on fundamentals, short form games, and long form scene work. Some games are described in the A to Z section and others deserve attention, especially for video improv.

Introduction: Set the tone at the start of the session with clearly defined boundaries. Make sure everyone knows it is a safe space for everyone to participate without fear of sexism, racism, homophobia, transphobia, ageism, ableism, and hate speech. This is also the time to share pronouns and if there are any particularly triggering topics that the group should refrain from mentioning or discussing. This is an opportunity for social distraction and play time in a safe and friendly environment.

All players and participants are assigned a number (1-10+). This will help determine talking order when speaking during certain activities. Zoom can be difficult if people "talk over" each other. Assign "first come", alphabetically, random, or however you wish as long as it is clear who/where each person is in the group order.

Here is the set list of our first ZoomProv session along with some tips of how to make it effective.

WARM UP:

-Pick Two
Stand up! All players will move in and out of their camera box, dancing and moving around. If only two players seen in the gallery view they "high five" and cheer. Body movement!

-Alphabet Square
Sequentially go through the alphabet. A category is provided to go around one word at a time A to Z and/or Z to A. Real or made up words. Go quickly and as accurately as possible. If a letter is skipped, it becomes the new reality of the alphabet. Just get the team used to speaking through Zoom and going around the square.

-10,9,8 things
The first player has to quickly list 10 things (any category) and then they challenge someone to list 9 things of a new category. Then challenge someone else to list 8 things...etc. Go around until everyone gets the chance to participate. Categories should start broad and progress to very

specific. (10 foods you love...1 reason to fear commitment)

-Word Association 2-deep

Get a random word from anyone. That is the beginning word. Follow the pattern and continue around the zoom sequentially. Keep the responses to a single word or very short phrase.

Example: Peanut butter. Player 1: "Peanut butter" makes me think of "jelly". "Jelly" makes me think of "jam". Player 2: "Jam" makes me think of "dunks". "Dunks" make me think of "Michael Jordan", etc.

Do this for 2 rounds. It's helpful and important to stick with the structure.

-Group Mind

Take the last word of Word Association round 2. Can the group guess what word is coming up next? Any player can say "one" and any other player can say "two". On a count of "one, two, three" both players will say their word. If the words match, you have group mind. If the two words are different, take the two words that were shared and seek a bridging word. Keep going until you find group mind...or chaos since its zoom.

-Zip Zap Zop

Call out the name of the performer to Zip/Zap/Zop also pass along a facial expression in the cam

"Steve" Zip, "Stephen" Zap, "Freeto" Zop

Other Variations:

Colors or Words (Red/Blue/Kiwi)

Noun, Verb, Adjective

Short sentence (Example: Stephen Freeto/eats pineapple/ on pizza)

Combine all (zzz and variations) "Zip/Blue/on Pizza"

ALL PLAY (Games for everyone)

-185 or any pun game

Go in order with no skipping. Force yourself to come up with a pun): random noun (I call my sweetie, sex with us, Hey Morty, B Movie, or any pun related line format.

-Press Conference

One person hides their eyes/ears (or is sent to a breakout room. Various software features may make this easy) while the suggestions are determined. Other players can write something on paper and share it with the zoom screen or use the chat feature. That player is having a press conference. They are someone famous and they did something (invented, arrested, or why they are infamous). All other players ask leading questions to get the person to guess who/what. Offer characters and personalities when asking questions (name and media outlet).

-Word at a time story

Tell a story one word at a time. Get a genre and a title. Start with "once upon a time"

-1 Minute Ted Talk

One person gives a 60 second motivational or informative presentation.

-30 Second Monologue

One person starts a monologue and continues for 30 seconds. After 30 seconds the monologue continues with the same tone and same concept with a new player. Continue with other players. You may need someone to show a timer to the zoom.

-Poetry: Each player presents a piece of poetry based off a suggestion or single word. Free verse, couplets, limerick, haiku, etc.

-Yearbook

Get a suggestion for a "high school club" (improv club, yearbook, etc.) Each player freezes in their camera box. One at a time, players will introduce themselves in character and say something about the club, themselves, or others.

Character Work

-Classic pairs

First player will introduce a brief character

Second player will add a "classic pair" to compliment the first player. All players will clap and proclaim "Classic Pair".

TWO PLAY (Games for 2 players)

-Ding (say it again, say what)

One person has a bell or makes bell sound (simply say "ding"). Upon a ding of the bell, rephrase what was just said. Alternate version "New Choice": host requests "new choice or say what or say it again" to change the words, accent, emotion, etc. The host can ding the players or a fun variation is to have the players ding each other.

-Actors Nightmare

One person can only read from a "book". Other person must maintain the conversation and justify what is being stated. Use a novel, text messages, Facebook, twitter, or any written words.

-2 Heads 1 Voice

Players play a scene every other word or at the same time.

-Two Person Scene

Get an opening and closing line of dialogue. Using one sentence at a time create a scene. Establish who, what, where...

-Dear So and So

2 Players will have a pen pal relationship (suggestion needed). Players will write a short letter (reading it aloud while writing) back and forth to each other. First player read their letter..."Dear so and so... and ends with love whoever". Make the letters short, interesting, and heightened.

-3 Act Play

Act 1 (2 Characters in a setting or event) Use only facial expressions

Act 2 (Same 2 Characters 20 mins later) Single word conversation

Act 3 (Same 2 Characters 20 mins later) Single Line of Dialogue

TWO PLUS (NOT ALL)

-First line last line

Get an opening line of dialogue. 2 players start a scene. Say freeze to stop the scene. 2 other players will start an unrelated scene using the last line of dialogue from the other scene. Continue using the last line of dialogue to switch back to the other scene. The characters and the plot of the scenes continue.

-Pillar/Hesitation

Start a scene between 2 players. A pause (hesitation) will prompt a third player to provide the next word (single word). "Third player" will rotate sequentially through remaining players.

-Numbers: Assign each player a number which represents the number of words they can speak.

-Superhero Wedding Best Speech

Similar to superhero eulogy but we want to keep it positive. Superheroes are getting married. Two players will do a "best man" or "maid of honor" speech. (Gender norms and heteronormative expectations are not required. Marriage is between 2 (or more) loving people.)

LONGER FORM

-Free Form
Use any location, relationship, or suggestion from the session to "cut to" the scene. Use characters and edits (time hop, etc.)
-Scene paint
Each person adds an element of the scene. Start with simple suggestion and each person adds to the element of the scene. Add objects and characters but no plot. Once the scene is painted, start the scene remembering and recalling what has been painted.
-Two person scene-start in the middle. Focus on emotion. Be affected by the emotional response.

- Every scene should have some object work.
- Go vague to clear. But still answer who, what, where.
- One line at a time. (Think about what happened, what was said, object work and everything that just happened before responding.)

- Rushing to get to the end you will miss stuff. Slow down take time to appreciate the scenes.

-Make it worse 1-10

Actors play a scene and each time the director shouts the next larger number (starting from 1 going to 10) the actors have to make the situation worse for the characters (on a drive 1. We're lost. 2 were out of gas. 3. I hear something in the bushes 4. The baby is coming! 5. I want a divorce 6. Whatever was in the bushes is getting closer 7. Eat my husband! 8. The baby is here! It's a vampire baby! (You cheated on me with a vampire?) 9. Here's my secret vampire lover. 10. Aliens!)

-4 Part Character

First player offers a name, second player offers an adjective, and the third player offers a profession. The fourth player then improvises a thirty-second monologue as "Harvey the paranoid waiter" (or whatever.)

Other Ideas:

- Overdub or voiceover a tv show: show a muted tv or movie clip.
- LaRonde: Character 1 meets character 2. Character 2 meets Character 3. Character 3 meets 4...etc.

- Character Interview: Pick a character from the session and interview that character.
- Practice job interviews.
- Work on social skills.
- Mute the mic and speak for each other.
- Have a conversation.
- Book an online therapy session instead of doing improv.

ZoomProv may be the future of improv, indeed. Back in December 2019 we had a dream, maybe even a premonition. The future of improv for GoProv would be unlike anything we've ever done. GoProv was boldly going where no other team has gone before. The theme of "Game On: The Future of Improv" was meant to be a nod to the very distant future of cyborgs, robots, and SpaceProv. Thank you Ben for designing a great image of the future. The season was meant to be a series of game shows and mixed form of short games, long scenes, a projector, a movie screen, and all of the technology available at our place. Fast forward to March 2020...the world shuts down. No live performance, no theatres, no face to face interactions, and only the internet connecting people. Well, well, well, our imaginary future of robots and technologically advanced screens became the only source for improv. The future is now. We are learning to improvise using computer, cell phone, Zoom, Twitch, Facebook live, IG live, and every new app available. It is different indeed, but many of the rules and guidelines apply. A rule for GoProv and friends is "if it's not a hell yes, the answer is no." Get people who say "hell yes" and make sure everyone is participating because they want to be involved. It's the only way to embrace the changes and the new normal. Plus Zoom has a mute button.

Image credit: Benjamin Longcor

Go, ZoomProv!

Chapter 5

Audience Interaction

Audiences...who needs them, right?

It's easy for an audience to take control of the suggestions, the show, and the tone. Do not let them! Give them some ability to contribute but please know that it will get dirty real fast. If you are in a place that serves booze, there will be chaos and booty references as the night gets later. The cruder the audience, the less fun it will be for the players. Get right to the edge of the line and do not let the players cross it. Let the audience go there in their mind while everyone on stage maintains a little bit of dignity. Figure out what works for you and your team. Sometimes you want something specific from the audience and you can guide them there, other times you may only need a simple word or phrase. You do not have to take the first thing you hear. Just know that the drunk and rude people are the loudest. An epic GoProv moment was with a drunk guy in the crowd who was interjecting and getting laughter from his interruptions and comments. This guy and this situation needed to be handled. We called him up on stage and did a quick interview. We got his name and where he works along with some other details. At that point we had already played some games where players had to leave the stage area to be called back shortly. We told him he had to go away for the scene and we would call him back in a minute. Oops, we forgot to call him back. Eventually he realized what was up and at that point he sat back down, quietly. I don't know if someone talked to him while he was gone or if he felt guilty for being obnoxious.

When you bring an audience member onto your stage, treat them with respect and make then look great. Even drunk dudes like to be complimented, just don't give up the focus or the control.

When asking the audience for suggestions (aka ask for), say the suggestion you don't want to use in your scene. For example "Hey, we need a job for this person. What is a career that they can do that isn't proctologist, gynecologist, or librarian?" GoProv is tired of playing scenes in a library or about a below the belt doctor. You may end up with something gross like politician or something else but at least it's creative.

Be careful with your phrasing and your words. One time we asked for a favorite type of writing, expecting to get romance novel, comic book, teen vampire, choose your own adventure, or something like that. Instead, we got an epic response...Cursive! Thanks Kendra. It was a beautiful moment. We had to play a scene in cursive. We could have ignored the answer but we chose to see what it would look like to do a scene in cursive. I can't remember anything else about the scene, but we asked a question, got an answer, and made magic. That answer was so magical and memorable that we did a show the next season called GoProv: Now in Cursive. Ah yes, good times.

Once the troupe has a good rapport and you know that they trust each other, you can just get a single word suggestion. Smart players will take that suggestion and dig deep to find a reference somewhere in the bucket of ideas that is fresh. What does that suggestion make you think of? And what does that make you think of? Explore that.

The suggestion "bucket" makes me think of KFC which makes me think of the musician "Buckethead". Look it up. It's real and if you are the only one who gets that reference then play it strong enough that people think you are weird, hilarious, or hilariously weird.

Love your audience. Make them look good. Invite them back. Give away tickets if you have to fill the house. Share the love of improv.

Go, Improv!

Chapter 6

Long Form

Let's call this the Alanis Morrisette chapter. Isn't it ironic that including long form in this collection is making the book too long? So, it's being cut. I will offer some tips for now. Maybe there will be a sequel to this book with more focus on long form.

The Harold...is a fantastic art form. It deserves its own book. GoProv has dabbled with long form and short form. Together it's a "medium form".

The guidelines for long form apply to short form, so let's just remove the descriptions of long form styles and include these helpful tips. Now that you have read about the guidelines and worked on some short form games. Use this information to keep building your improv foundation.

- You are an improviser. You are an actor doing a show without a script. You are not a comedian. Be funny by creating humorous scenes. Remember to discover.

- React honestly. This takes listening skills. Listen and respond with an honest reaction. Even if you are playing a character or an animal or something inanimate, you can react in an honest way.
- First 3 lines: The first 3 lines are the most important of the scene (or edit). These lines have to establish the scene in a seamless way without being overt.
- 3 Gifts: There are 3 gifts that we can offer throughout, especially the first 3 lines. Gift of scenario establishes what is going on in the scene, Gift to self is endowing yourself with who or what. Gift to partner endows your scene partner with the "who" or "what" needed to keep the scene moving.
- Each scene should have an action, marrying action, gift, and an emotional response. Having these items along with one of the 3 gifts, the scenes will be more complete.
- Being witty is not everything. An audience will appreciate a well-developed scene. Humor that occurs naturally goes a long way.
- Establish who, where, what as quickly as possible in a seamless manner and remember who, where and what is going on throughout the scene.
- Conflict in a scene is good, however we must agree on the circumstance. Acceptance of

the circumstance is most important. Conflict is different than denial.

- Commitment and specificity will greatly improve every scene. Commit to what you are doing and be specific in your words.
- Opening lines with huge emotional responses get the audience interest and help establish the scene. Remember to have action, marrying action, gifts along with emotional response.
- Start in the middle without immediately introducing who/where. Show and state something that moves the scene forward.
- Establish a past. Have a shared past with scene partners.
- Show don't tell. Object work is important. Taking time to establish the setting will allow you to share with the audience without having to talk or explain. Just remember what you have established.

Check out these long form styles

Harold, Maestro, Armando, Assscat

And so many more.

Go check out the social media presence of improv comedy teams, troupes, and theatres. It is a great community to share and learn.

Go, Improv!

Chapter 7

Directing an Ensemble

Good improv looks easy. Bad improv is hard to watch. End of chapter.

en·sem·ble
/än'sämbəl/

noun

1. 1.
   a group of musicians, actors, or dancers who perform together.
   "a Bulgarian folk ensemble"

2. 2.
   a group of items viewed as a whole rather than individually.
   "GoProv is an ensemble"

To really produce a good improv show, your ensemble should work closely together to form a relationship, a rapport and a bond with each other. Not having a script ensures the unknown will happen, so do whatever it takes to help the team bond. When players know what each other likes, hates, is capable of, and how they perform the overall performance can exceed expectations. GoProv is full of inside jokes, especially on stage. Players through the years have such a bond and connection that there is joy in pimping your fellow players. Setting up a player for a huge laugh because you know they have a character that will fit the scene or you know they have some knowledge of something obscure is important. Getting to know each other off stage, in the green room, or after hours is a great way. Talk shop, talk life, make stuff up, build your circle of trust, and make friends!

3,2,1 Go, Improv!

Chapter 8

Showtime

Find a way to follow these P's and E's

- Protect your players: give them support, have their backs.
- Pay the creatives: if you can, give creative people some reward for their time, their talent, and their efforts.
- Pander to the audience (to a degree): make the audience happy but don't let them run the show.
- Push away the bullshit: No reason to accept bullshit suggestions like gynecologist, proctologist, etc.
- Energy: attack that stage and keep building momentum. Finish right before you peak.
- Excitement: Show up! Do what you say you will do. Share your events. Bring friends. Joyousness is best.
- Equality: Make sure everyone is treated with respect and given the same opportunities to be on stage.

There is such an excitement to perform in front of an audience. If your troupe has the option of choosing where to perform, make decisions that are going to set you up for success. GoProv has played some very awkward venues. Initially we would never say no to a gig. This put us in bars, in churches, in barns, in a Church/House (Chouse if you are from Goshen), on the football field of a school, at a conservative republican college, and so many non-traditional locations and venues.

We quickly learned that performing in a bar where the improv show is not the highlight of the night turned into a competition with college kids drinking booze. Make sure you get paid for these gigs. You do not have to play for free. Your time and your talent has a value.

GoProv has been very fortunate to have Art House as our home base. It has been a partnership that I will forever be grateful.

If you have seen a GoProv show you will know that we have a wooden stool that we name and assign for each season. After each performance all of the performers would sign a section of the stool. This is a GoProv tradition. If you have signed the stool, I want to thank you for being a special part of my life. Thank you for being a friend.

Go, Improv!

Chapter 9

Inclusivity in Improv Comedy

There are so many relevant subtitles for a chapter titled "Inclusivity in Improv Comedy". Here are just a few to help emphasize the specific intent of this piece:

- The Do's and Don'ts of inclusivity in improv
- It's not just for middle aged white guys anymore
- Producing an improv environment free of toxicity
- How to identify, discuss, and stop racism, sexism, ageism, hate, and ignorance on the stage
- Move out the way, you toxic white male
- No, the female of the group does not have to be pregnant or a stripper or a pregnant stripper on stage
- Racism is not funny
- Ok, calling all toxic white women "Karen" is funny

Acceptance, followed by the heightening of the offer is one of the most basic and generally accepted "Do's" of improv. Being endowed with "character traits" including relationship, age, and profession help move scenes along. Suggestions of gender, race, or ethnicity are not necessary. Getting a suggestion of a location or an occupation is the fuel that improvisers need to allow them to "yes, and" the scene and their teammates. Most likely leading to an unpolished and mediocre scene with just a few laughs (come on now. It's true. Not all improv is funny or good). Quite possibly the laughs come at the expense of the marginalized members of our society. Almost all audiences will provide "gynecologist" and a male player will hold his back, spread his legs, and give birth to a beautiful white baby. Simple and easy laugh to earn even though we've seen it a million times. Be creative and unique with your choices.

Let's start with players who identify as "male" and "female". Most likely a male player will endow a female player with "mom" or "prostitute" or some other antiquated gender stereotype. Improvisers know the rule of acceptance, so as a good player you have to "yes, and" those offers, right? There is no need to answer that question. Let's stop it before it starts. Enough white male dominance. This is true for improv comedy and the rest of the world actually. The audience suggestion, the performer's initiation, and the start of the scene is what we should focus on first. Don't accept it.

Don't play it. Don't do it. Train the audience to be smarter. Don't reward them with sexist, racist, ageist, and intolerant kibble by accepting these suggestions. Be better. Start before they sit down.

Know your performance space and the venue. Quite simply encourage and assist theatres, venues, and facilities to have Inclusivity and Diversity statements. See the Goshen Art House Statement for reference. Do not perform at a place that does not have these beliefs or standards. Post it publicly. Let patrons know that the space is welcoming to all and there is no place for hate. Make the statements visible and more importantly make sure everyone who works, volunteers, or walks through the doors knows and lives by the policy. That was easy.

Now that the space and the audience knows the requirements and beliefs, it's vital to cast a diverse group. No more all white male majority. Do not form or maintain an improv group or team of all white males. You are not Monty Python or any other famous all white male comedy group. Don't even try. Seek diversity. "It's only white dudes that show up to auditions" is no longer an excuse. Actively fix it. Do not cast all white guys. Seek members of the community that are diverse. Actively recruit and include all people regardless of race, socioeconomic class, color, national origin, religion, diverse perspectives, age, sex, sexual orientation, gender, gender identity, neurological or physical ability, veteran status, legal status, or education level. Focus on diversity in the cast. Take away the straight white male presence and I bet the group will be more comfortable and perhaps more funny.

Before you create an audition notice, focus on informing yourself about privilege, marginalization, cultural appropriation, gender identity, pronouns, common definitions, and basic human rights. Art has always spoken about the struggles of those underrepresented and mistreated. Even though it is a stretch at times to call improv "art", it is important to know that your "art" should be helping and not hurting.

Yes, you can make and publish Inclusivity Statements. Yes, you can bring awareness to issues in the greater community. Yes, you can be edgy and "controversial". All of this can be done without stepping on the existence of others, especially those that are traditionally underrepresented or marginalized.

The Do's of a troupe/team

- Do have a diverse cast.
- Do discuss the inclusivity and diversity requirements.

- Do provide a safe opportunity for all to share their pronouns (frequently).
- Do require a contract from players to honor, respect, and live the Inclusivity Statement.
- Do offer a safe place to gather, to play, to participate, and to spectate.
- Do offer a confidential and neutral point of contact for conflict resolution.
- Do give space for all to share and express their needs.
- Do everything possible to remove toxicity.
- Do treat everyone fairly.
- Do keep learning, evolving, discussing, and growing.
- Do "do run run".

The Don'ts of a troupe/team

- Do not allow behavior that does not follow the written and shared policies, procedures, guidelines, statements.
- Do not assume gender or pronouns.
- Do not be complacent.
- Do not be jerks.
- Do not give stage time to jerks (performers or audience members).
- Do not "do run run", actually.

The Do's of a performer

- Do know the difference between "Race", "Ethnicity", and "Nationality".
- Do form a friendship with your teammates. Get to know them and share yourself.
- Do respect and honor your teammates.
- Do know the boundaries of your teammates and respect them.
- Do step out of the way if you can make room for someone under represented.
- Do your work before getting on stage (improv can be therapeutic but not at the expense of your fellow performers).

The Don'ts of a performer

- Don't endow players who identify as women with gender stereotypes. (Why use "mom" when you can use "doctor", or "Captain" or something more interesting.
- Don't endow players of color with stereotypical names that relate to a specific culture.
- Don't use a voice or accent that mocks a race or ethnicity.
- Don't appropriate a culture. Learn what this means before taking the stage.
- Don't, just don't.

Definitions

Diversity: Extent at which an organization has people from diverse backgrounds represented throughout. It is a recognition of individual differences: race, ethnicity, age, gender, gender identity, expression, sexual orientation, physical abilities, nationality, language, religious beliefs, and socioeconomic background.

Equity: The state, quality or ideal of being just. Applying the principles of fairness and ethics to a given circumstance or set of conditions.

Inclusion: Equal access, well-being, and a sense of belonging for all members of the organization.

Additional Definitions

TheyDiffer.com describes the distinctions between race, ethnicity, nationality, and culture:

"While all of these refer to the distinction of one community from another, they do have differences.

"**Race** refers to a group of people who possess similar and distinct physical characteristics ... such as skin color or hair type. In other words, race constitutes a human population that is distinct in a way from other human groups based on their physical differences, imagined or not."

"**Ethnicity** or ethnic group refers to a category of people who regard themselves to be different from other groups based on common ancestral, cultural, national, and social experience. ... One must share a common cultural heritage, ancestry, history, homeland, language/dialect, mythology, ritual, cuisine, art, religion, and physical appearance to be considered as a member of an ethnic group.

"**Nationality** pertains to the country of citizenship meaning it generally refers to where a person was born and holds citizenship. It is the legal relationship between a person and a sovereign state.

"**Culture** is the way of life that consists of the general customs and beliefs of a particular group of people. It generally means the non-biological or social aspects of human life, which is basically anything that humans learn in a society. A bit similar to ethnicity, but is often used to refer specifically to the symbolic markers used by ethnic groups to distinguish themselves visibly from each other."

Cultural appropriation otherwise known as cultural misappropriation is the adoption of an element or elements of one culture by members of another culture. This can be controversial when members of a dominant culture appropriate specifics from disadvantaged minority cultures.

GoProv Code of Conduct

• Both on-stage and off, performers, directors, students, and teachers are expected to treat hosts, fellow performers, participants, audience, and the playing space in accordance with the Code of Conduct.

• Respect physical boundaries. Do not hit, shove, lift, tackle, or otherwise place yourself or others in the way of physical harm.

• Respect sexual boundaries, on and off stage. Do not grope, simulate sex, touch sexual areas, or be otherwise sexually aggressive toward others.

• Ensure that you have consent before engaging physically with your classmates or fellow performers.

• Create and maintain a harassment-free environment. Harassment includes but is not limited to unwelcome sexual attention, deliberate intimidation, inappropriate physical contact, offensive comments relating to race, gender, religion, or identity, and encouragement of any of the above behaviors.

• There will be zero tolerance for hate speech including racism, sexism, homophobia, transphobia, and xenophobia.

• Be each other's advocates; Help everybody have fun and engage in the joy of improv in a safe, supportive atmosphere.

- Continue to listen, learn, grow, develop, nurture, and participate in a safe environment to share the joy of improvisation

Anyone who is abusive, bullying or harassing, or otherwise violating any of the terms of the Code of Conduct may be asked to leave our venues and may be barred from returning and performing again.

A confidential "third party" will receive and address any complaints and concerns presented by all visitors, participants, performers, teachers, directors, leaders, and guests.

There will always be a level of oppression in the world. How we address it and work against it is what matters. We all have bias and we all make mistakes. Sometimes in improv your words move faster than your thoughts. If you acknowledge the areas that you need to address and actively put forth the work you will be a better improviser and a better human. There's a phrase in comedy that may be a relevant reminder: Always punch up and never punch down. Make fun of those with a higher status instead of making fun of someone with a lower status. Punch up if you have to punch.

Go, Improv!

Chapter 10

Do Good Art

In the year 2020 a momentum turned into a movement. Years and years of discussion of how to be better at handling racism, sexism, hate speech, and how to make change all happened during a pandemic. We have to stop and talk about how to be ANTI...antiracist, antisexist, antifascist, and be better as a creative human. Believe it or not, improvisers are indeed artists. An improv audience can get rowdy, can be inappropriate, and can be IST...you know sexist, racist, and all the other important marginalized groups that deserve protection and fair treatment.

Here is a concept that GoProv will be trying soon. We plan to give some power to the audience to pause a scene for discussion. Obviously this isn't meant to happen after every scene, but there are times when something comes up that may need discussion. It's improv, there are no trigger warnings or a way to know what is offensive to an audience. Obviously, the players need to play at the top of their intelligence and be respectful to each other, the audience, marginalized people, and to members of society who are under-represented.

A real example of an opportunity to discuss a scene: During a GoProv show, one of the players portrayed a kid at Disney. Because of the short form nature or the scene, the character was not fully developed or identified. The performer made a choice of the physicality of character in which an audience member was offended by the choice. After the show via messenger, the audience member reached out to discuss what was viewed as an ableist choice feeling as if a disability was the joke. Imagine being able to discuss choices, intent, and perspective with an audience member after the scene versus not having that discussion or having it much later after the show. There has to be a way to have a discussion especially about racism, sexism, ableism, and other important topics. This could be helpful for the players to learn and share with the audience. The point is to make sure you are willing to discuss how to be better. How to be inclusive, how to be anti...anti all the things. Create art, make laughter, and be better. Right? As esteemed one term First Lady Melania once said on the internet "Be best".

Improv is life. Life is complicated. Improv is complicated. It is also a joy to form a circle, trust your mates, make someone smile, and make things up. That sweet spot between fear and joy which we all know as improv gives us reason to get on stage and be alive.

Shout out to the cast of *Whose Line Is It Anyway*, Laura Gouin, Judy Fabjance, Charna Halpern, Del Close, your mom, Heidi Tack, and audience members far and wide. Much love to Amy, Hannah, Olivia, and even Peggy. I am thankful for your support. Here are some GoProv folks that are amazing: Pipp, Steph, Aaron, Greg, Geoff, Alex, Caroline, Jason, Adam, Julie, Angel, Charlie, Kelli, Alyssa, Katie, and hundreds more. Thanks to Sadie for helping me with the "woke" chapters. Thanks to everyone for helping me understand that I do not always know what I am doing but I certainly know that we will figure it out sometime right before or right after the black out. In the early days, I would lay in bed after a show thinking about what I could have said or done differently. It would drive me crazy wishing and hoping I was better. Now I know to stay in the scene that I am in and do what I can with what we have. Focus on the right now not what just happened or what will happen. Improv is life and everything is a gift worth getting.

Now, you know what I know.

Go, Improv!

Tell them The Freeto sent you